DAY STARTERS
FOR COUPLES

45 DEVOTIONS
FROM GOD'S HEART TO YOURS

David & Claudia Arp

FaithHappenings Publishers

FaithHappenings Publishers
7061 S. University Blvd., Suite 307
Centennial, CO 80122

Cover Design: ©Angela Bouma
Book Layout ©2013 BookDesignTemplates.com

Day Starters for Couples © David and Claudia Arp –1ˢᵗ edition
ISBN: Softcover: 978-1-941555-06-4
This book was printed in the United States of America.

To order additional copies of this book, contact:
info@faithhappenings.com

FaithHappenings Publishers,
a division of FaithHappenings.com

CONTENTS

Preface vii

1. Canopy of Love 1

2. A Constant Love 3

3. In Sickness and in Health 5

4. Heart Talk 8

5. A Path in the Snow 10

6. Light in the Darkness 13

7. Enduring Love 16

8. New Beginnings 18

9. The Making of a Marriage 21

10. A Steadfast Love 24

11. Angels in the Snow 26

12. Viva La Difference 28

13. A Crisis Call 30

14. Time for Marriage 32

15. Do You Want a Better Marriage? 34

16. Splendor in the Alps 37

17. Embracing Change 39

18. Unlimited Love 41

19. The Marriage Garden.. 43

20. Choose Faithfulness.. 46

21. The Simple Life... 48

22. Ten Minutes a Day 50

23. The Time Is Now.. 53

24. Be My Lover Bunny 55

25. On Top of the Clouds.. 57

26. True Love 60

27. A Legacy of Love 62

28. Called Together 64

29. Two-Part Harmony... 67

30. Just the Two of Us 69

31. Til Death Do We Part.. 72

32. Extravagant Love... 74

33. Breaking for Life.. 77

34. The Marriage Tree 79

35. Call Unto Me... 82

36. In Pain and In Joy 85

37. Follow the Light 87

38. Courageous Risks... 89

39. Seize the Day 91

40. Monday Morning Coffee 94

41. Unfriendly Skies.. 97

42. Slow Down, Be Renewed............................ 100

43. The Gift of Love 103

44. A Prodigal Marriage 106

45. The Sands of Time.................................... 108

Preface

In the beginning God created man. He created them male and female. He created them in His image. And to this day a husband and a wife who love God and love each other can reflect God's image to a hurting and broken world. You can be such a couple if you learn to listen and follow the quiet whispers from God's heart to yours. It's a wonderful way to stay each day as a couple.

Perhaps in the past, you've felt His presence—that gentle nudge, an impression, a soft reminder... almost an audible whisper from the very heart of God that helped you refocus and renew your love and commitment to each other.

We believe that if we really listen with our hearts . . . we can hear His quiet whispers in our everyday experiences. That's what this little book is all about—learning as a couple to discern God's voice and following His leading.

Won't you join us as together we view a kaleidoscope of loving couples who, in the midst of their joy and pain, learned to hear God's gentle whispers? Our prayer is that in the quietness of your heart you, too, will hear His voice—that you will experience God's touch and reflect His love to those around you.

DAVID AND CLAUDIA ARP
DECEMBER 2015
WWW.10GREATDATES.ORG
WWW.FACEBOOK.COM/10GREATDATES

ONE

Canopy of Love

Weddings: times of celebration—times of joy— and times of new beginnings. Each wedding is special but this particular wedding, for us, was unique. Julia and Tim were to be married under a canopy. The canopy, taken from the Jewish wedding tradition, signified God's protective covering for the bridal pair. Flowers and ribbon graciously adorned the tulle canopy under which the couple would soon stand to take their vows.

Julia, so strikingly beautiful in her elegant yet simple wedding dress, floated down the aisle on her father's arm.

We had known Julia for many years and had watched her grow up and transition through the adolescent years to womanhood. Now she was about to commit herself to love, cherish and partner with Tim for the rest of her life.

We thought of the changes just ahead. In a few weeks Tim would begin law school. Their life would be hectic, busy and full—very, very full. We prayed silently that God's canopy of love would protect them; that God would guide them; that they would remain faithful to their vows they were about to take.

Then a gentle nudge came from God's heart . . . *Pray too for your own marriage and the other marriages represented here today. Pray that those who have been given this trust of marriage might prove faithful. Pray that you will keep living out your marriage under my holy canopy day by day.*

He has taken me to the banquet hall, and his banner over me is love.
SONG OF SONGS 2:4

TWO

A Constant Love

It's early morning on a spring day. The sun's rays are quickly chasing off the fog. The water in the bubbling brook and the wild flowers peeking thought the snow greet two hikers. They are college students, desperately in love, cherishing precious moments together. Following the Smoky Mountains trail up and down the hills, they attack the rough terrain, while in the valley below the brook widens and the musical sound of the rustling water fills the air. The majestic mountains tower above.

The lovers stop frequently to embrace. At the trail's end the blaring, boisterous water leaps over Abrams Falls and drowns out the couple's concerns and fears. Hand in hand they pledged their love . . . *Our love for each other will flow just as constant as this waterfall for as long as we both shall live.*

Leap forward four decades. Years have passed but the path to Abrams Falls is unchanged. It's another beautiful spring day. The lovers on the path are now parents and grandparents. They walk more slowly but just as intentionally. Hand in hand, they steady each other over the rough places. Years of the trials of living have gone by, but still in love they slowly traverse the hills and valleys. Stopping to rest, they embrace. They kiss and remember stolen kisses here on this path so many years ago.

Once again they listen to the roar of Abrams Falls. They watch the sparkling water cascade over the rocks, smooth from centuries of contact. So much in life has changed, yet Abrams Falls seems the same. The same rocks, the same towering mountains, the same rushing water, the same peace.

Suddenly they realize they are standing on holy ground. Reverently, they listen, and their Heavenly Father, the Creator of Abrams Falls, the Creator of love, speaks in a small, still voice: *The beauty of nature and the ability to love is my gift to you. Your love, which has endured the rapids and waterfalls of life, is your gift back to me. Embrace. Kiss. Cherish and celebrate your love in the afternoon of your lives.*

You are always new. The last of your kisses was ever the sweetest.
JOHN KEATS

THREE

In Sickness and in Health

The honeymoon suite was romantic, complete with heart-shaped spa and a dozen red roses. Definitely a great setting for our twentieth anniversary celebration. But it was not to be—at least not on this particular anniversary.

We took one last longing glance at the room just waiting for us to enjoy it, grabbed the vase of roses, closed the door and got back in our car. Then we drove the hour back home. Our youngest son had come down with the flu.

Later that evening as we munched our anniversary pizza, we remembered how, years ago, we had pledge to love each other in sickness and in health. We were so young. I (Claudia) was barely twenty. I (Dave) was twenty-two. Two college students, desperately in love . . . and afraid that Khrushchev, the head of the

Russian Empire, was going to blow the world up. It was during the Cuban Missile Crisis. We were afraid we would never get to live together as husband and wife. So we did it. We got married right in the middle of college.

Well, the world didn't blow up and over the years, and we have had many opportunities to love each other in sickness and in health—both our illnesses and those of our three sons! And here we were again . . . another disappointment. More cancelled plans. Another opportunity to live out our marriage vows. And then we realized . . . *that's what marriage is all about—supporting and loving each other when things work out and also when things don't work out. We had vowed to be there for each other in sickness and in health, for richer or for poorer, and for better or for worse.*

Marriage is a package deal. The good comes with the bad. Health, sickness, times of abundance, times of need, times things are great, times things are lousy—all are part of the fabric of marriage. And while it's much more enjoyable to love in health than in sickness, both are vital if we want to have a growing and lasting marriage.

So on that anniversary, home with our sick son, we informally renewed our vows. We looked at our roses, cuddled on the couch and watched a romantic movie. Perhaps next year we'd try again for the heart-shaped spa. Meanwhile, we would love each other in sickness and in health.

There is surely a future hope for you, and your hope will not be cut off.

PROVERBS 23:18

FOUR

Heart Talk

"He is the love of my life and I know I'm the love of his," Megan said. "But my husband rarely expresses his love in words. Basically, I say it and Chris thinks it."

"Does this bother you?" we asked.

"Not really," Megan replied. "I decided a long time ago I didn't want to miss connecting to him just because I'm a talker and he's not, so I don't nag him or demand a lot of talk. I try to enjoy the shared silence."

Megan speaks from experience—she and Chris just celebrated their twenty-fifth wedding anniversary—twenty-five years of marriage history.

In their early twenties, they started a trucking business. Before the kids came along, they trucked together. "We would go for miles and miles and Chris would say nothing." Megan said. "At first it bothered me. I'd bait him for complements and conversations, but the more I persisted, the quieter he became. Long periods of ice-cold silence. Each of us was missing the other's expectations. Then one day it hit me: *listen to his heart—don't demand his words.*"

As we listened to Megan, we thought, *What difference would it make in our own relationship if we concentrated on listening to each other's heart and not emphasizing the words or lack of them?*

Would we give each other the benefit of the doubt? Would we express our love in non-verbal ways—a glance across the room, a hug or kiss? Would we seek to affirm the other, instead of waiting for the other's affirmation? What would happen if, just for today, we only listened to each other's heart?

My heart is ever at your service.
WILLIAM SHAKESPEARE

FIVE

A Path in the Snow

The rays of the sun danced on the pristine snow as the gondola rose higher and higher. All was quiet, except for an occasional thump as we passed under another supporting tower. Below us majestic evergreens laden with snow bowed silently in reverence.

Reaching the summit, we disembarked. A breathtaking panorama of the majestic Austrian Alps surrounded us. We felt as though we were standing on holy ground.

The spell was broken when I (Claudia) said, "Dave, how are we going to get back down to the bottom? It's so steep!"

"Obviously," I (Dave) answered, "we're going to ski down. After all, that's why we took the twenty-minute gondola ride."

Years ago, skiing had been our family's favorite sport—but that was years ago. Now, we were venturing out once again. Out of practice, our ski legs—though weak—were determined to hit the slopes—as long as we hit them slowly.

It seemed to be a perfect day for skiing. Swish! Swish! We began our descent, stopping often to enjoy the beauty of it all. And with each successful turn, we became more confident—until halfway down the mountain we ran into fog. Thick fog. Pea-soup fog. This was not part of our plan! Pleasure was replaced with panic.

"What are we going do to now?" I (Claudia) asked.

Clueless, I (Dave) answered, "Pray!"

Together we considered our options. We could side-step down, but in the thick fog others might crash into us. We could take off our skis, carry them and walk down, but even then, not knowing the slope, we might get lost.

As we wrestled with our options, another couple— skiing at about our pace—skied by, and stopped just below us. Their laughter and obvious lack of concern assured us they knew the slope. They weren't gripped with fear like their two American observers. So as they skied into the fog, we bravely followed them. When they turned, we turned. When they stopped to rest, we stopped to rest. Without realizing what they were doing, they safely guided us safely down the mountain.

Answered prayer? Definitely! Angels in ski suits? Probably not, but they could have been! Unknowingly, they had modeled for us and provided a path in the snow for us to follow. Then it struck us . . . *others are watching us—what are we modeling?*

While we aren't the best models for traversing and getting down ski slopes, we began to realize that couples may be following us in other ways. What about younger couples who pattern their marriage after ours? Or the couples in our small group who watch how we handle difficult situations, or how we deal with conflict, or even how we handle success? Yes, others may be watching us right now and be influenced by how we relate to each other. Are we being good models?

What about you? What difference would it make if you knew others were watching you? In our confusing, foggy world yours might be the only marriage model others see clearly. It's something to stop and think about.

Glorify the Lord with me; let us exalt his name together.
PSALM 34:3

SIX

Light in the Darkness

For Doug, it was just a routine check-up with the dermatologist. The doctor said removing the small mole was preventative and nothing to worry about.

Then the phone call—would Doug come back in? The doctor could see him at 3:00 PM the next day.

The following afternoon Doug and his wife, Cindy, sat across from the doctor. "Doug, the mole was malignant," the doctor said. "You have melanoma." He paused for a moment, then continued, "I've made an appointment for you with a surgeon. He will do some tests, and we'll go from there. We caught it early. And that's positive."

Doug and Cindy looked at each other. Positive! How could cancer ever be positive? Numb, confused, scared and riddled with anxiety, they listened as the doctor tried to reassure them.

Later that evening, after getting their three young children in bed, they held each other and vowed to get through this crisis together. They considered the future. What was ahead? Surgery? Radiation? Chemotherapy? Often the greatest stressor is dread—the fear of what might happen. Would the cancer spread? Would Doug die?

In the middle of their fears, they prayed, "God, we don't know what to do, but our eyes are upon you. Please give us your comfort and your peace and see us through this crisis."

Later that night as they read from the book of Psalms, God comforted them and addressed their fears . . . *Even in darkness light dawns for the upright . . . He will have no fear of bad news; his heart is steadfast, trusting in the Lord. (Psalm 112:4, 7)*

In the coming weeks Doug, with Cindy at his side, got through the surgery. The doctor removed the lymph nodes and they prayed that the cancer had been caught in time.

At times Doug was strong. Other times he was fearful and Cindy carried the load. Waiting several weeks for the final lab report was a dark time for both of them. Then the good news: "Your lab report came back negative," the doctor said.

Sometimes things work out well as they did for Doug and Cindy. Other times God gives the grace and comfort to get through the bad news. If, like Doug and Cindy, you choose to focus on God and trust Him in the darkness, you don't have to live in fear. Whatever the future holds, He will see you through it. The darkness of your situation will not be so dark when you follow God's light.

The stars are constantly shining,
but often we do not see them until the dark hours.
EARL RINEY

SEVEN

Enduring Love

As we ate dinner with marriage enrichment pioneers David and Vera Mace, we were intrigued with the way they looked so tenderly at each other. Could a couple who had been married over forty years still have the spark?

Yes, and it was contagious! We were in the North Carolina mountains with several other couples for a week of training. As the Maces talked with the group that evening, it was almost as if the two were speaking as one.

Later that night, we knew we had found a living model of what we wanted for our own marriage. Could we have such a vibrant marriage after we had been married for forty or fifty years? Then in a quiet nudge the answer came: *Yes, but now is the time to decide what you want your marriage to look like in the future.*

For the rest of that week we reflected on what we wanted our marriage to look like when we were in our seventies . . . our eighties . . . and if God should grant us more years together, in our nineties. What did we want to characterize our relationship on our fiftieth wedding anniversary?

Now, more decades have gone by. Time for another check-up. What progress have we made? What dreams are yet to be fulfilled?

Now is the time to decide what our marriage will look like in the future!

Commit to the Lord whatever you do, and your plans will succeed.

PROVERBS 16:3

EIGHT

New Beginnings

The raindrops drummed the same boring cadence on the windowsill, not unlike Liz and Mark's ho-hum relationship. Sitting across from the counselor, they knew their marriage was in trouble—filled with broken promises, missed expectations, lost dreams.

Liz and Mark had met in college and married right before Mark started medical school. Liz put her own academic plans on hold and worked in retail to help get Mark through med school. But those years of hard work and struggling to make ends meet transitioned into years of affluence. Mark just been asked to join a prestigious medical group. To others, it appeared they had it made. They were on "easy street." Then why were they so miserable?

True, their lives were opulent and affluent with things, but their relationship was impoverished.

Houses, cars and "stuff" didn't bridge the chasm in their relationship. They needed help. That's why they were here, but was it too late?

"When a long-term marriage crumbles," the counselor said, "usually it's not the result of a major crisis or a one-time event. Like your experience, little things build up over the years. It's easy to disconnect emotionally. But a relationship is much easier to put back together within the framework of a marriage. It's up to you. You can choose to reconnect, to rebuild your relationship and to start over. Are you willing?"

Mark and Liz looked at each other. Each knew the answer should be *yes*, but they had no emotional reserve—no strength left to verbalize it. The hurts and disappointments were deeply embedded. Could they really start over? Silently they looked at each other . . . if only they could go back years ago when they lived in poverty, when their relationship was abounding in love. Slowly Mark reached for Liz's hand . . . they touched, and suddenly there was a glimmer of hope. Was it really possible—a new beginning? Then, it was as if God whispered to their hearts: *Yes, this can be a day of new beginnings. What is impossible with man is possible with me. I will make all things new!*

"How do we start?" Mark asked the counselor. Liz nodded her head in agreement.

"Let's start," the counselor said, "with the One who created marriage in the first place. Let's commit this process to God and ask for His guidance, strength and help."

Together they bowed their heads. "Father, we come before you this afternoon," the counselor prayed, "to ask for your strength for Mark and Liz. Give them the courage to forgive each other, to release their hurts and disappointments, to focus on the future, and to rebuild their marriage. Now, please guide us in this process and make this a day of new beginnings."

Liz squeezed Mark's hand. Their eyes locked. Both knew the road ahead would not be an easy one. "You don't solve in one day what took years to develop," the counselor had told them. But deep in their hearts, they knew with God's help it was possible to start over. This was, for them, indeed a day of new beginnings!

Forgiveness ought to be like a canceled note—torn in two, and burned up, so that it never can be shown against one.
HENRY WARD BEECHER

NINE

The Making of a Marriage

At a neighborhood party Kelly asked in frustration, "Can you tell me what a healthy marriage looks like? I want to make my marriage work, but life is so hectic with four kids under six, there isn't time. Besides, I don't know where to start."

Others joined our conversation and a lively discussion followed. What are the characteristics of a healthy marriage? The group mentioned commitment, faith in God, good communication, romance, and common goals. But if we had to put it in a nutshell, we'd say, "A healthy marriage is one in which there is a willingness to find time to work on your relationship."

"Great," Kelly said. "But with four kids and a part-time job, do you think I can really find time to work on my marriage?"

"Yes," I (Dave) answered. "But you have to be intentional."

According to a poll of twelve thousand people, the number one cause of marriage failures is simply not working on your marriage. No one plans to be a divorce statistic, but life happens, relationships slip, marriages break up. But the news isn't all bad—the number one cause of divorce is preventable!

We took our own informal survey and asked people, "Why don't you work on your marriage?" And the overwhelming answer was "lack of time."

It takes time to grow a healthy marriage and we have to continually look for moments to invest. We've been working on a marriage for decades, and time and time again we still have to regroup, reprioritize, and free up moments for each other. And when we get too busy, God is faithful to remind us. In the midst of our business, we hear His loving nudge. . . *It's time to slow down, to take time to talk, to reconnect, to invest in your relationship.*

And when we experience His gentle nudge, we put on the breaks. It's the way to avoid trouble up ahead and to keep our relationship going in the right direction.

Stand at the crossroads and look; ask for the ancient paths, ask where the good way is, and walk in it, and you will find rest for your souls.
JEREMIAH 6:16

TEN

A Steadfast Love

The gentle breeze coming through the open window laden with geraniums was a welcome guest on this late spring day as we lunched with our old friends. Markus looked tenderly at Renate as he helped pull her sweater over her shoulders.

For the past fifteen years she had been in and out of hospitals interspersed with days, months and years of no energy, poor health and little hope of ever being well again. The doctor's puzzlement as to the diagnosis of her condition was a chronic frustration, as were their unanswered questions and prayers to God for healing and strength.

But today we were celebrating. At last, some of Renate's strength had returned as evidenced by our lunch together at this lovely, old farm restaurant. As we thanked God for the delicious food we also thanked him for Renate's improving health. Then we asked how they had survived the last fifteen years. Markus answered, "We took life one day at a time."

Renate continued, "God has been so good to us. We've learned so much about his faithfulness. My illness has actually brought us closer together. We don't know what the future holds, but we have peace day by day as we know that God *will be with us in sickness and in health.* We know he holds the future and that he is watching over us."

No complaints. No bitterness. Fifteen years of struggles, yet no evidence of anger. Privately, we wondered how we would handle life if we were faced with similar difficulties?

Later that afternoon after we said good-bye to our friends we got in our car and headed back to our hotel deep in the Black Forest of southern Germany. As we traversed the curving mountain roads we struggled with our own lingering questions. In the silence we found answers as God whispered to our hearts, *Don't fear the future. I will be with you—in sickness and in health.*

We could never be brave and patient if there were only joy in the world.
HELLEN KELLER

ELEVEN

Angels in the Snow

At last the children were in bed and asleep. We quietly slipped out the front door of our chalet. Time for us. Time for a short walk and a breath of fresh air.

How close the stars looked! The diamond-studded sky illuminated the snow-covered path.

Walking together in the snow was a great way to end a fun but exhausting day. We had spent the day teaching our youngest son how to manage the rope tow ski lift. And our two older sons still needed supervision. Ski vacations at this stage of family life were not that relaxing. But now was our time. A few minutes to be alone. To walk and talk in the snow . . . to refocus on us. With three small kids, focusing on us was harder to do.

We missed the carefree days when "fun" was an integral part of each day. Now we were "the parents" and too often "the serious parents." We had come a long way from our carefree dating days.

As we walked in the snow I (Claudia) asked Dave, "When you were a kid, did you ever make angels in the snow?"

Before he could answer, I just did it! I lay down in the pristine snow by the side of the road and made an angel!

Dave broke into laughter and joined me. We made a whole platoon of snow angels. As we laughed at ourselves, we promised to never completely grow up.

As if giving His seal of approval, our Heavenly Father seemed to say to us . . . *take time to play, to be childlike, to enjoy the beautiful world I created for your pleasure! Don't take yourself so seriously.*

We looked at each other, and Dave threw the first snowball. This was one fight we both won.

Years later, we still remember that night of hugging, kissing and playing in the snow, and we still remember God's whisper to never completely grow up—to take time to play and to enjoy God's wonderful creation called *life.*

How great is the love the Father has lavished on us,
that we should be called children of God!
I JOHN 3:1

TWELVE

Viva La Difference

We sat across the table from Zoe as she answered our interview questions. Our assignment as part of the International Year of the Family at the United Nations in Vienna, Austria, was to interview people from as many different nationalities as possible to discover the positive things that families were doing around the world.

Zoe was one of the most delightful people we talked to. She was from Brazil and was married to a German. Two radically different cultures; yet their marriage seemed to work. We wanted to discover their secret, and as Zoe began to talk, we did:

"Hans and I are radically different. He's organized and likes structure. Without him I would be a mess. I'm the spontaneous one and, I must admit, I'm a random person. My motto is 'Que sera sera—whatever will be will be!'

"When we first were married, we didn't get along that well. Our different cultural backgrounds complicated our relationship. For instance, Hans expected us to eat dinner at six each evening—just like clockwork! My desire was to have dinner when we were hungry and certainly not before eight or nine. I didn't want to get in a boring routine.

"Then we began to realize that God created each of us unique. If we trusted Him, He could mold us together as one, with the best from each benefiting the other. Now our relationship is great. Our differences give texture to our marriage. Hans keeps us organized and focused, and I, well, I liven things up!"

The twinkle in Zoe's eyes validated her words. This very different cross-cultural marriage worked. Their secret? In our hearts we knew . . . *let your God-given differences enhance your relationship.* It's one secret smart couples know.

Accept one another, then, just as Christ accepted you,
in order to bring praise to God.
ROMANS 15:7

THIRTEEN

A Crisis Call

The phone rang. I (Dave) answered. On the other end was my director. Would I teach at an upcoming conference in West Virginia?

Actually, it wasn't *would I?* It was "You will be there!" But there was a dilemma—Claudia was very pregnant with our third child, and the conference was to be in a remote mountain retreat center. There was no quick way to get home in case the baby came early or Claudia needed me.

I was perplexed. If I were really spiritual, my director insinuated, I would trust God with my family. The director needed me at the conference. I prayed and pleaded with God to change my director's mind . . . but He didn't. Still no resolution—just a brick wall.

Finally, alone on my knees, I cried out to God, "If you aren't going to change him, then please show me what I'm supposed to do." Silently, I waited—and then in the quietness, I suddenly knew what I had to do. Almost in an audible voice, God spoke to my heart . . . *Dave, there will be many other conferences in which you will teach, but only one opportunity to be present at the birth of your baby.*

Later that day I told Claudia, "I'm not going to the conference—even if I get fired."

We both felt God's peace and I knew I had made the right decision. Amazingly, our baby was born a couple of weeks early—at the exact time I would have been away at that conference. And amazingly, my director accepted my decision. He didn't fire me and I kept my job.

For me, that was one of those defining moments when I chose to make my marriage a priority. Since that time Claudia has never doubted that she and our children come first!

Things don't always work out that well. Since that time I've experienced other really difficult situations where God did not whisper such a clear answer. But over the years I learned that when God doesn't remove roadblocks, in time He will show me ways to go around them.

Call to me and I will answer you and tell you great and unsearchable things you do not know.
JEREMIAH 33:3

FOURTEEN

Time for Marriage

Totally exhausted, we sat in our car glaring at each other. "Why do we do this to ourselves?" I (Claudia) asked.

I (Dave) answered. "I really don't know, but something has to give!"

We had just finished giving a program on dating. But we couldn't remember our last date. And on this evening there would be no "on-the-way-home-stop-off-for-coffee-date." We still had to finish and send off the corrected manuscript for a book we were writing on how to build a creative love life. Some lovers we were. On that evening we would have settled for a love moment—let alone a love life!

We had become so consumed with helping other couples that we were in danger of letting our own relationship slip. Of course we rationalized, "Helping others keeps us working on our own marriage." Yet on that evening as we raced to meet our deadline, we knew in our hearts we were wrong. Where were the boundaries between our work and our marriage?

Late that evening after we sent off our manuscript, we both agreed to make some changes. At that moment we knew . . . *Our work will wait while we grab some time for our marriage, but our marriage won't wait until we finish our work.*

We knew we needed to make some changes. Together the next day we looked at our upcoming schedule, as painful as it was, we cancelled some discretionary things on our calendar so we could add some margin for us. Then we planned several days away just for us.

And now, even years later, when the boundary between work and marriage begins to get fuzzy, we declare a marriage evening. We leave electronics off, send calls to voicemail, light a candle, put on soft music and celebrate our marriage!

Give us, Lord, A bit of sun, A bit of work, And a bit of fun.
ENGLISH PRAYER

FIFTEEN

Do You Want a Better Marriage?

John, a successful surgeon, had his life all mapped out—his practice, his golf and his family. Sarah, a dedicated mother and community leader, seemed focused and settled in her life as well. Then one day Sarah asked John, "John, what do you really want out of life?"

She was totally unprepared for his answer, "Sarah, I want our marriage to be better!"

Looking at each other in shock, they began to talk about their relationship. Before long they realized . . . *We can have a better marriage if we want it!*

Together, they began a journey that would span more than two decades and would lead them to a deeper, more satisfying relationship. Their success is recorded in a letter to us written just before John retired. Let us share part of it with you:

> *Dear Claudia and Dave,*
>
> *In reviewing our thoughts on our forty years of marriage, we asked ourselves what discoveries we felt we'd made, what we'd learned, and how we feel as we close this chapter of our life and begin our adventure into retirement. By far, the biggest discovery was that we should change and can change! At first change was very threatening, but when we became involved and discovered we could, it became exciting.*
>
> *We had to relearn how to listen to each other... Becoming better listeners, being more honest, more careful, and more companionable, we learned much about ourselves and about each other. Also, we developed more trust and reliance on each other as we learned how to work together.*
>
> *Finally, we feel we have reinvented our marriage relationship, in a manner compatible with this stage of life. We look forward to the next chapter of our life together with great optimism and enthusiasm...*
>
> *Best of friends,*
> *John and Sarah*[1]

Like our friends the McCrackens, all who are willing to choose to work at it *can* have better marriages!

---

[1] Letter excerpted from Arp & Arp, *The Second Half of Marriage* (Zondervan, 1996). Page 205

The development of a really good marriage is not a natural process.
It is an achievement.
DAVID AND VERA MACE

SIXTEEN

Splendor in the Alps

Walking hand in hand through the silent woods, we paused to appreciate the beauty. With the backdrop of towering Alps, the snow-laden ever-greens reminded us of a favorite calendar on the wall in our home office. The majesty of God shouts from every mountain peak, but how easy it is for us to miss it back at home when we get too busy.

So as an antidote to our own busyness, and a cele-bration of making it through yet another year, we are here at our favorite hide-a-way in Obendorf, a little village tucked away in the Austrian Alps. Here to re-lax, here to write, here to reconnect with each other.

Here is it is easy to feel God's presence—to hear his voice . . . *Slow down and enjoy my creation. I am the one who formed the mountains, the trees. Each snow flake is an original design. I also created you. Take time to acknowledge me and walk together on my path. It's the path of blessing.*

We pause and thank God for helping us through another year and for giving us this moment of peace and tranquility.

Let us encourage you, wherever you are, to pause and appreciate God's handiwork. You may not walk through the snow, but you can turn off the electronics and appreciate the silence, or stop for a moment to look at a sleeping baby, or watch a sunset or smell a flower.

Remember God created it all. Let him help you slow down. He is the One who stills the roaring of the sea and waves. He waters the land with rain and makes the crops to grow. If God's power is so awesome in nature, can't we also trust Him with our lives and with our marriage? It's something to think about.

They will speak of the glorious splendor of your majesty,
and I will mediate on your wonderful works.
PSALM 145:5

SEVENTEEN

Embracing Change

Room by room, we slowly walked through our family home for one last time. Our words echoed off the empty walls as we randomly grabbed memories from two decades of family life. "Dave, do you remember when we first found this house and there was the ice-maker hook-up we needed and had prayed for?" I (Claudia) asked.

We smiled at each other, remembering how years ago we had scraped together our pennies for the down payment, and how that ice-maker hook-up in some strange way had confirmed that this was to be our home!

"Yes," Dave replied. "And remember how huge this house felt when we moved here with our two pre-schoolers?"

Our children grew up in this house. Now all three sons were gone, and the real estate sign in our yard read "Sold." We were saying goodbye to our wonderful family home that had too much yard and too much room for just the two of us. Reality hit. We were moving. Our life was changing.

We were actually entering a new stage of life: a time to downsize—a time to refocus. What lay ahead? With apprehension, we closed the door of our family home for the last time, walked down the sidewalk and got into the car.

We knew God would go with us into the unknown future. With His help we could surmount the empty-nest challenges—to share our dreams, to make fresh commitments and to work toward a more satisfying union. Together we would embrace this new season of life.

As we backed out of our driveway for the last time, our hearts were comforted with an unspoken thought . . . *Change is as certain as the seasons. Embrace it! I will go with you.*

Pulling into the traffic, we turned at the next the corner. Our future awaited us and with God's assurance, we could face it with optimistic enthusiasm. The rest just might be the best!

Life has taught us that love does not consist in gazing at each other but in looking outward together in the same direction.
ANTOINE DE SAINT-EXUPERY

EIGHTEEN

Unlimited Love

Perhaps you have heard the story of Robertson and Muriel McQuilkin. He served as president of a Christian college and she, also very gifted and articulate, worked in media.

Then the unthinkable happened. Muriel's memory began to fade and became increasingly worse. The day Muriel was diagnosed with Alzheimer's their lives changed forever. Their forty-two-year marriage would never be the same again. But what did not change was Robertson's commitment to love his wife in sickness and in health. He was still several years from retirement, and as the disease progressed, friends encouraged him to put Muriel in an institution. He simply would not consider it and told his friends that in an institution, no one would love her the way he did.

When we heard this story, we looked at each other and wondered how we would respond in a similar situation. Would God give us the grace to remain faithful? Could we bear the pain of watching the other slowly decline? Could we deal with the mood and personality changes that accompany Alzheimer's? How would we cope?

Then in the middle of our fears and our questions, God whispered to our hearts . . . *My grace is sufficient for you. Whatever you may walk through, I will go with you. My faithfulness endures forever.*

God forbid that we—or you—would ever have to walk the same path as Robertson and Muriel McQuilkin. But if the unthinkable happens, we can be assured that our Heavenly Father will give us the grace to remain faithful to each other. While God may not lead you to quit your job as he led Robertson McQuilkin, you can know that He will go before you and show you the way you should go. Remember that His grace is sufficient and His faithfulness endures forever.

For great is his love toward us,
and the faithfulness of the Lord endures forever.
PSALM 117:2

NINETEEN

The Marriage Garden

The rows of young corn plants resembled a military marching band with the tassels swaying in the late afternoon breeze. Rain was in the forecast. As I (Claudia) hurried to finish weeding, I could picture our family sitting around the table eating corn on the cob dripping with melted butter. Yum!

My vegetable garden was my pride and joy. For the past five years we had lived in an apartment in Vienna, Austria. So to have a yard again was great. But the real treat was having my very own vegetable garden, and soon corn from it would be on our table!

Then the storm came. High winds. Thunder. Lightening. Inches of rain. Early the next morning we surveyed the damage. The rows of corn were now in disarray. It looked like a herd of cattle had trampled through our garden.

"Dave, it's just not fair!" I cried. "I worked so hard and now my corn is ruined."

"Not to worry," Dave said. "I'll get some string and stakes and we'll tie the plants back up."

After hours of hard work, we survey our garden. Each corn plant was now a prisoner securely tied to a stake. About that time our neighbor, Carol, who was a seasoned gardener, came over, looked at our tied up corn plants and burst into laughter. "Why on earth did you do that?" she asked. "Don't you know when the sun comes out, the warmth of the sun's rays will cause the corn to straighten up?"

We looked at each other. Muddy, tired and exhausted, we realize we had worked in vain to do what nature would do on its own. We needed to work with nature—not help nature out. We really couldn't control the weather, and we couldn't control our corn plants. But God, who created nature, had it all under control.

How foolish we felt. Later, when we reflected on our gardening experiences, we realized that it's just as foolish to try to manipulate each other. To get all tied up trying to fix and control everything about each other. Sometimes we need to let God's sunlight do the correcting. Yes that was it. At that point we understood . . . *our Heavenly Father is the gardener of our marriage. He sends the rain and the wind and He sends the sunshine. His healing power will make our relationship grow.*

So what happened to our garden that year? In our attempt to save our corn, we unintentionally packed the soil and disturbed the plants. We had some corn, but the plants never quite recovered. The next year we saved our string and stakes and let the sun take care of things. We also tried to be more sensitive with each other. Like our garden, our relationship requires a lot of work and attention. We need to shower each other with support and encouragement. And when our marriage gets hit by the storms of life, we look to God and ask Him to send warm rays of healing. We want to keep cultivating our "marriage garden" so that in the future we can reap the fruit of a healthy relationship.

The garden is the place where we discover that faith is a work of art.
HARRIET CROSBY

TWENTY

Choose Faithfulness

A glance across the room. Eyes lock. Chemistry. Unwanted chemistry—but there just the same. Jake thought of Lynn—his love, his wife for over a decade. What was happening?

And then deep within his heart, he felt the silent nudge . . . *Flee! Go! You have a choice. Choose fidelity. Choose faithfulness. It is the path of blessing!*

Without looking back, Jake walked out of the room, grateful to God for his gentle nudge. On this day Jake chose the hard road of faithfulness and fidelity.

In today's world, temptation seems to lurk behind every corner. Have you felt it—a sudden attraction to someone other than your spouse? A look, a random touch, a listening ear on the day your partner was deaf? If you haven't, chances are you will. So let us encourage you—when it happens, listen for the gentle whisper, *Flee! Go! Choose faithfulness; it's the path of blessing.* You'll be glad you did.

Do not let your heart turn to her (his) ways or stray into her (his) paths.

PROVERBS 7:25

TWENTY-ONE

The Simple Life

On a late spring day, we slipped away for a cup of cappuccino at a little sidewalk café on the edge of a lake. The water glistened in the afternoon sun. As we sipped our coffee, we watched the ducks splashing in the water. All was calm and peaceful.

Nearby, we observed a young family, complete with a baby in a stroller, also enjoying the ducks. Suddenly, the baby threw her pacifier to the ducks, and an amazing thing happened. The ducks began to fight over the pacifier. First the mama and papa duck fought for it. The winner would swim around, pacifier in mouth, until the other duck would swipe it away. Then the little ducklings got into the act. Each was determined to win the pacifier, which of course was useless to them. We laughed at how ridiculous the ducks looked with that pacifier in their mouths.

Then we began to think . . . *aren't we sometimes like those ducks? Don't we struggle to grasp things that we don't need? How much time do we spend chasing useless things that we think will pacify us?*

It's a fallacy to believe that "the one with the most toys wins." Things never have and never will satisfy. Without realizing it, sometimes we are as silly as those ducks. Then a penetrating question: *"What fruitless goals are you chasing? What are the pacifiers of your lives? Are your priorities out of order because of your desire to have things that don't really satisfy?"* We realized it was time to re-evaluate our lifestyle—time to consolidate and simplify.

We left the sidewalk café with a new zest to invest in the important things of life and in the future. The ducks can have the pacifiers!

Who lives content with little possesses everything.
NICOLAS BOILEAU-DESPREAUX

TWENTY-TWO

Ten Minutes a Day

Alone at last, Steve and Jan looked at each other across the candle-lit table. The old Italian restaurant was a perfect setting in which to celebrate their twelfth wedding anniversary.

I wasn't sure we were ever going to get here," Jan said. Then she rattled off how she had coordinated—piano lesson, homework, and she had even found another dad to sub for Steve at soccer practice that evening.

"Now that you brought up soccer," Steve said, "I'm concerned about the lack of parental support for the team."

Jan then mentioned the problem with Hannah's kindergarten teacher—and Joey simply could not start nursery school until he was potty-trained.

Over dinner the conversation moved from the kids to their budget. As usual, money was tight. "As a matter of fact," Jan said, "We should head home and relieve the babysitter."

Later back at home, after putting Joey to bed—the babysitter couldn't get him to sleep—Jan and Steve snuggled on the couch to watch a movie. But after a few minutes, both fell sound asleep. Some anniversary.

Then next morning, Jan and Steve rehashed the night before. Even after overcoming mountains of obstacles to celebrate their anniversary, they had spent most of the evening focusing on the kids, finances—everything but their relationship.

"We used to be best friends, soul mates, lovers," Jan said. "Now it's more like we're running a business—a family business. We keep saying things will change, but nothing does."

"There's always a crisis—at work or at home—and we just seem to run out of energy and time before we get to us." Steve added.

Discouraged, they looked at each other. And then they
realized ultimately, it was up to them to make a change. In the silence, the answer came . . . *It is never too early or too late to make changes! Today, you can choose to make your marriage a priority.*

That morning Steve and Jan made the choice. They agreed to try a thirty-one day experiment. For the next month they would carve out ten minutes a day to focus on each other. Whether early in the morning before the kids woke up, or in the evening after the kids were in bed, they agreed to spend ten minutes together and acknowledge it as their couple time.

During those thirty-one days, they faithfully claimed their couple time. Even in those times when they were too tired to talk, they invested ten minutes holding each other and sitting close to each other. Did it make a difference?

"Yes," Steve told us. "It was just a little step—just ten minutes a day—but we proved that little steps, if taken in good faith, can change everything."

Time is a very precious gift of God;
so precious that it's only given to us moment by moment.
AMELIA BARR

TWENTY-THREE

The Time Is Now

Time—what is it? Sixty seconds makes a minute, minutes turn into hours, and hours into days. Time zips by almost unnoticed. Then something happens and time seems to stand still. Life is never the same again.

It was one of those phone calls you dread. Lillian, Dave's mom, had suffered a stroke. In the next few weeks as she lingered between life and death, time stopped long enough for us to reflect on this remarkable woman and the seasons of her life and marriage.

Dave's parents were married for fifty-five years. As we reflected on their years together, we thought about our own marriage and a challenge . . . *Are you being good stewards of the time you still have together? How are you investing your marriage moments?*

Each season of marriage comes with different stress points and challenges. The casual discovery days of the first months and years accelerate into the hectic parenting years and on into the empty nest and the retirement season of life. The years quickly race by.

As we considered my parent's fifty-five year marriage, I (Dave) remembered how, when I was a young boy, my parents from time to time would go off alone together. As a teenager, I'd catch them hugging and kissing on the balcony. I remembered how as empty nesters, they were each other's best friend. Throughout the seasons of their marriage, they took time to love each other.

Now Lillian is gone. We realize anew that our marriage is time-bound and someday we too will be parted by death. We ask ourselves, *are we being good stewards of the time we do have?*

THE TIME IS NOW

If you are ever going to love me,
Love me now, while I can know
The sweet and tender feelings
Which from true affection flow.
Love me now while I am living.
Do not wait until I'm gone
And then have it chiseled in marble,
Sweet words on ice-cold stone.
If you have tender thoughts of me,
Please tell me now.

ANONYMOUS

TWENTY-FOUR

Be My Lover Bunny

Jeanie smiled at her husband, Dave. "From the beginning of our marriage, we've had fun together. Even when the children came alone, we still managed to find time for each other."

"Not as much time as before kids, but we always found some time," Dave added. "And that didn't end when we entered the empty nest. We simply filled our nest with bunnies!"

When we visited in their home, sure enough, rabbits were everywhere! They even have four stuffed bunnies who travel with them. But their fun relationship is about more than bunnies. That's just the beginning.

Jeanie told us. "For years we've had pet names for each other—not just two or three—we have hundreds!"

"What's your favorite?" I (Claudia) asked.

She answered with a smile, "Lover Bunny."

They also have special kisses. They send each other love letters. At airports they fake good-bye kisses and then get on the plane together. And at the grocery check-out counters, Dave often asks Jeanie to marry him all over again.

Their light-heartedness influences other areas in their relationship—even areas of conflict. Years ago they came up with the ten-minute silence rule. At any time, either can call for ten minutes of silence. If the nonverbal is a problem, they also have an out-of-sight-for-ten-minutes rule. This helps them calm down and get things back in perspective.

What has kept this couple's fifty-plus-year marriage happy and delightful? In our hearts we know their secret . . . and then we heard the confirmation . . . *Fun and laughter is a key to a great marriage . . . Couples who play together, stay together!*

And Dave and Jeanie are the living proof!

If a man insisted always on being serious, and never allowed himself a bit of fun and relaxation, he would go mad or become unstable without knowing it.
HERODOTUS, THE HISTORY OF HERODOTUS, BOOK II

TWENTY-FIVE

On Top of the Clouds

The illuminated seatbelt sign reinforced what I (Claudia) already knew—we were flying through turbulence. I checked the security of my seatbelt. When the weather is sunny and the winds are calm, I like to fly. But on days like this one, I'd rather have my feet on the ground.

And how was Dave handling all this turbulence? Looking over at him, I was simply amazed. He was actually sleeping! I desperately wanted to wake him up. What if it got worse? What if we hit wind shear?

As I tried unsuccessfully to relax, I began to think about how flying in planes is similar to building our marriage. Over the years of our marriage, we've lived through turbulent times. Every marriage experiences turbulence. Of course, you want to avoid severe and extreme turbulence if at all possible. And while some marital turbulence can be avoided, at times you simply must fly through it. Unfortunately when some couples experience problems, their marriages crash and burn. We've dedicated our lives to helping couples avoid martial disasters—so what could I learn from this mental exercise?

About that time the pilot came on the loudspeaker and said, "As you are aware we are experiencing turbulence. For the next few minutes it will continue to be bumpy, since we are flying right on top of the clouds." *Oh,* I thought. *On top of the clouds!* I began to relax a little bit now that I knew to expect a few more bumps. And with each bump, I tried to picture our plane skipping on the top of the clouds.

Suddenly I understood: *it is possible to handle your fears of flying in bumpy weather or even turbulent times in a marriage if you know they are coming and if you stay on top of them!*

The key is to stay on top of the clouds! Later, when Dave woke up (refreshed and unconcerned) I told him about the turbulence he missed and the pilot's comments and my analogy. Our conclusion? The only way to avoid turbulence in marriage is to stay on the ground and go nowhere. And there are those static, boring marriages that do. But for couples who realize a little conflict is a given and who want to fly through it, their love for each other can grow. As our plane finely landed, we agreed we wanted to continue to grow through our own turbulent times. And from now on, when I'm faced with a rough flight, I'll try to stay on top of the bumps!

You will keep in perfect peace him whose mind is steadfast,
because he trusts in you.

ISAIAH 26:3

TWENTY-SIX

True Love

We were desperately in love . . . *young love, true love, filled with deep emotion.* I (Claudia) was a freshman at Maryville College, which was located on the edge of the Great Smoky Mountains. I (Dave) was in my second year at Georgia Tech in Atlanta, Ga. Two hundred miles apart! But we remember one time when Dave drove up for the weekend. Time for just the two of us! Time to be together.

Slipping away from the college campus, we drove to Cades Cove in the heart of the Smokies. And on that day we visited the past—others' past. Cades Cove, untouched by "American progress," is a tribute to the first families who settled there so many years ago. We imagined the young couples, in love and struggling for survival in the beautiful but isolated valley. We stood together in the Primitive Baptist church and talked about how someday, we would speak our marriage vows in the little Methodist church in Ellijay, Georgia, where Claudia grew up.

Now, decades later we revisited Cades Cove. We went back to the Primitive Baptist Church and once again remembered those lovers who went before us. We remembered our own wedding day now so many years ago.

We talked about the future and wondered what the future would hold for our grandchildren. Would they ever experience the quietness and peacefulness of Cades Cove? Our world had become more complicated. Life was anything but primitive. How would they fare? And in the middle of our memories and fears for the future, God spoke to our hearts, *Never forget your past; let it enrich your present, but you must trust Me for the future. I am the same, yesterday, today and forever.*

And then we began to realize, the future—yet to be written—is in God's hands. Future generations will have their own unique love stories to write. But the greatest love story of all—God's love for us—will be the same yesterday, today and tomorrow.

Each happiness of yesterday is a memory for tomorrow.
GEORGE WEBSTER DOUGLAS

TWENTY-SEVEN

A Legacy of Love

"Thank goodness, this day is almost over," James said to his wife, Madison. Several weeks ago James' mother, after a lengthy illness, had passed on from this world to the next. Today's daunting task—clearing out her condo and going through her personal things—left them both exhausted and emotionally drained.

Now one more load to the dumpster. Throughout the day, they had sorted through her stuff—boxes and boxes of letters, newspaper clippings, old magazines and pictures of so many unknown people. Memorabilia others didn't want or care about. Junk that may have been precious to James' mother. As James threw away the last garbage bags, he stared at the dumpster and thought, "My mom's life is in that dumpster."

Then it hit him—one day that may be *my* stuff! *What heritage am I leaving to my loved ones—a dumpster of stuff, or a legacy of love and faith?*

Suddenly, James realized the choice was his. We also have choices to make. Os Guinness in *The Call* writes, "The trouble is that, as modern people, we have too much to live with and too little to live for. . . But for most of us, in the midst of material plenty, we have spiritual poverty. . . . Answering the call of our Creator is 'the ultimate why' for living, the highest source of purpose in human existence."[2]

Have you answered God's call? What is God's calling for your marriage? Do you need to invest in more stuff? Probably not. Perhaps what you really need to invest is more time. Time to declutter your lives; time to renew your love—long walks and talks. Precious moments invested in your marriage and family today will never end up in a dumpster tomorrow.

May your deeds be shown to your servants, your splendor to their children.
PSALM 90:16

I will surely bless you and make your descendants as numerous as the stars in the sky and as the sand on the seashore.
GENESIS 22:24

---

[2] Os Guinness, *The Call*. (Nashville: Thomas Nelson, 1998). Page 4.

TWENTY-EIGHT

Called Together

The plane touched down. We were on foreign soil. Switzerland. Our three small sons in tow, we deplaned. It was official—we were "foreign missionaries." Scared "foreign missionaries."

John, a fellow worker, met our flight and drove us into the city to a small three-room apartment over a store. As we looked around our drab setting we observed the basics: beds, a stove and refrigerator, four chairs and a table.

"Take your time getting settled." And with that John was gone. The one link to our own culture drove down the street and disappeared into the distance.

We were alone. We looked at each other. I (Claudia) cried. I (Dave) had no idea what to do. Our fifteen-month-old toddler was just beginning to toddle, and he kept stubbing his toed on the threshold at each door, each time falling down and crying—over and over again. Our four-year-old complained, "I'm hungry. I want something to eat!" Our six-year-old, said, "I miss my friends. I miss my room. I want to go home!"

Here we were—in a foreign country to help others—yet we were so needy ourselves! Our mission at this point was survival. (I) Claudia ventured to the store below our apartment. Somewhat successful, I came home with bread, milk and bologna.

Tired, exhausted, discouraged. Finally we got our boys to sleep. Sitting at the table, listening to the drizzling rain and the noisy street traffic, we looked at each other and cried to God for help. "God, did we misunderstand? Did we make a mistake? Why are we here?"

As we held each other, God met us at our time of greatest need . . . *You are here because I called you! Together you are here to serve me. I am faithful. I will do it. I will accomplish my will. I will never leave you helpless. Put your trust in me!*

Tears still flowed. Questions and uncertainty remained. But our Heavenly Father who held the answers comforted us. We could trust Him. Whatever trials, whatever adverse circumstances we must face, we could be confident that God is God and that He would be our God in this foreign and strange land. We turned off the light and went to sleep. Tomorrow was another day. Tomorrow was the future. God would walk through it with us.

> *Do not be afraid, for I am with you.*
> GENESIS 26:24

TWENTY-NINE

Two-Part Harmony

The logs in the open fireplace crackled a warm welcome to the guests who had assembled to celebrate the union of Marcy and Tim. Outside the snow continued to fall. The ambience of the old hunting lodge on this cold winter day was a wonderful setting for a wedding reception.

The small, intimate ceremony, completed just a few minutes earlier, had reaffirmed that God is the one who created the holy state of matrimony. Vows spoken. Two lives joined as one. Two hearts fused together in love. Now the celebration.

In the background the musical notes of a classical guitar and violin filled the room with romantic cords. Each instrument complemented the other. Wonderful two-part harmony! And then God seemed to whisper . . . *Marriage is a two-part harmony—each has your own notes to play. Play them in such a way that you complement and harmonize with one another.*

What a beautiful picture of a marriage! Two lives harmonizing together to create a new entity—a marriage. But too often we want to play our own song without harmonizing with the other. Or we want to be our own voice rather than blending together as one. Yet in a duet each seeks to enhance the other so that together the music is more beautiful than it would have been with just one playing or singing alone.

In a harmonious marriage there is no room for competition or tooting your own horn. Competing is the opposite of harmonizing. If we're playing in harmony, it means we mutually respect each other and our unique gifts. It really is like we are two different musical instruments playing different parts. With God's grace we can continue to make beautiful music together!

Do nothing out of selfish ambition or vain conceit,
but in humility consider others better than yourselves.
PHILIPPIANS 3:3

THIRTY

Just the Two of Us

We'll never forget that crisp, clear fall day when we dropped our last son off at college. He looked so young and vulnerable, but we knew he was ready to face the challenges that college life would present him. We weren't so sure about ourselves! Slowly we got in our car, backed out of the freshman dormitory parking lot, waved our last good-byes, drove out of the Wheaton College campus and began the ten-hour trip home.

As the miles went by, an unfamiliar cloud of silence descended. Usually chatty, Claudia was pensive; reflective; almost disoriented as we entered the uncharted waters of the empty nest. The first dilemma— I (Dave) wanted to take the slow road home. After all, what was the big hurry?

I (Claudia) wanted to get home ASAP and Lysol the house! But then what? Neither of us knew. So much of our lives had been consumed with parenting our three sons—actually our marriage and family ministry grew out of our love for family—but now what?

Working as marriage educators, we knew the divorce rate soars in the empty nest and that every marriage—including our own—is vulnerable. Each spouse faces unique challenges. Women must deal with menopause and the signs of aging in a "youth-oriented" world; plus they lose their major identity as mom. On the other hand, at this stage men often reach the peak of prestige. Their egos soar. I (Claudia) still remember how a few gray hairs made Dave even more attractive—and I wasn't the only woman who noticed. Definitely not a confidence builder!

So that fall as the leaves turned, we both turned to the One who created marriage. Looking at familiar verses through the lens of the empty nest, God filled our hearts with a new zest and excitement for investing in our own marriage and honoring him with the second half of our life. Our marriage verses Ecclesiastes 4:9-12 took on new meaning. . . *Two are better than one . . . and now we are two again. So let's embrace the empty nest.*

As we attempted to reinvent our marriage for the second half, we discovered that while we lacked energy and stamina, God blessed us with patience, experience, and balance. Together we worked to create a more partner-focused rather than child-focused marriage.

Now years later, our empty-nest journey continues. We're still learning to adapt to changing landscapes, but each fall as we watch the leaves paint the countryside with unrivaled beauty, we're reminded of God's provision for every stage of life. And Robert Browning's words are etched in our hearts, *"Grow old along with me, the best is yet to be."* With God's help, it will be!

Two are better than one, because they have a good reward for their toil. For if they fall, one will lift up his fellow.
ECCLESIASTES 4:9-10

THIRTY-ONE

Til Death Do We Part

The dinner was exquisite. The atmosphere, romantic. The setting? A thirteenth-century castle, set high on a hill overlooking the medieval town of Esslingen, Germany. Sharing this special evening were our friends, Dorothea and Dankfried. Between us, we had logged over sixty years of marriage. Over dinner we talked about what marriage must have been like in the thirteenth century. Then the conversation turned to the state of marriage today.

"What's happening to marriages here in Germany is disturbing," Dankfried told us. "Many couples—even before they say *I do*—lack the commitment to love each other for a lifetime!"

"In some of the more modern marriage liturgies," Dorothea added, "couples commit themselves to stay together 'until our love dies' instead of 'until death do us part.'"

A chilling thought—as chilling as the stone walls of that old castle! What causes love to die? What causes love to live? And then it hit us . . . *for love to last, you must give up other options! Exercising your commitment strengthens your love muscles.*

There, surrounded by history, we renewed our commitment to nurture our love, to stick together through thick and thin, to keep on accepting and forgiving each other, and as we vowed in our own wedding liturgy so many years ago, *to forsake all others!*

God stands fast as your rock, steadfast as your safeguard, sleepless as your watcher, valiant as your champion.
CHARLES SPURGEON

THIRTY-TWO

Extravagant Love

Five of the six couples I'm presently working with," a counselor told us, "are facing a medical crisis and can expect to lose their spouse in the next six months."

We were speaking at a conference on how to build a successful long-term marriage and this counselor challenged us. "For these couples, 'long-term' is a cruel joke."

Her comments made us stop and think. "If one of us had only six months to live, what changes would we make?"

A few days later we heard another story and decided not to wait until we just have six months to change our perspective. Bob and Betty had been married for forty-two years, and most of those years Bob pastored a small country church. They loved having their grandchildren visit and looked forward to their retirement years. Bob was planning to retire at the first of the year.

At first he hardly noticed the headaches, but finally he decided to go to his doctor. He couldn't believe the words he was hearing! "Bob, you probably have six months—perhaps eight."

Suddenly everything changed for Bob and Betty. What was so important last week, wasn't now. Heartbroken, they began to talk about their immediate future. Then Betty did something out of character for both of them.

They had always lived very modestly. However, recently Betty had received a small inheritance. What she did with her windfall was both unexpected and extravagant. She bought Bob a red Mercedes convertible! Every day she took Bob for an afternoon drive in the new red Mercedes. And when the weather was nice, she put the top down. With the wind in their faces, they chose to focus on the present and to leave their fears and worry at home. Betty chose to be extravagant with her love and to celebrate their marriage for as many days as God chose to give them.

When we heard their story, our hearts were touched and we asked ourselves, *Are we as extravagant with our love?* And then we knew in our hearts, *You can be! Start now. Celebrate your marriage. Love each other with abandon!*

While no red Mercedes convertible is in our foreseeable future, we are trying to be more extravagant with our time and energy. We're being more liberal with our compliments. We're planning more dates. Hugging each other a little tighter. Kissing a little longer.

How about you? Are you extravagant with your love? It's something to think about.

Life is short, and we have never too much time for gladdening the hearts of those who are traveling the dark journey with us. Oh, be swift to love, make haste to be kind!

HENRI FREDERIC AMIEL

THIRTY-THREE

Breaking for Life

We sat in city traffic anxious to get home. The next day we were leaving for a series of conferences, and once again we were in the panic mode—too much to do and too little time!

Why do we always do this to ourselves?" I (Dave) asked.

Staring at the brake lights of the car in front of us, I (Claudia) replied. "I don't know, but I do know something has got to give. We simply can't keep us this pace!"

About that time on a voice in our car asked, "Are you experiencing 'fast-lane stress' in your marriage?"

We looked at each other and in unison said, "Yes!"

The radio spot that day seemed customized for us. We continued to listen. "If you're experiencing fast lane stress, here's a tip for you. Sit down and make a list of all the things you need to do. Then prioritize your list. Put the most important thing first and start there. You may not get everything done in one day, but you will go to bed at night knowing you have invested your time in doing the most important. Think about this—life is too precious to hurry through it."

The last seven words changed our day. It was as if God audibly spoke to us . . . *Dave, Claudia, your lives are too precious to hurry through them! Slow down and trust Me!*

As the traffic began to move once again, we knew what we needed to do. We drove straight home and over two cups of coffee we made our list and prioritized it. Then we divided the most important things that needed to be done before we left the next day.

The results? We didn't get everything checked off our lists, but we stopped hurrying. On that day we realized just how precious life is and how much we valued our marriage. And we vowed in the future when we get in a hurry to remind each other to slow down. By the way, what we heard that day on our car radio was our own two-minute program, *The Family Workshop,* and the couple we were listening to was ourselves! Sometimes we even take our own good advice.

We may run, walk, stumble, drive, or fly, but let us never lose sight of the reason for the journey, or miss a chance to see a rainbow on the way.
GLORIA GAITHER

THIRTY-FOUR

The Marriage Tree

Sitting with our friend, Vera Mace, on the screened porch at her home in Black Mountain, North Carolina, we commented that she and David must have enjoyed rocking on their porch and looking at the magnificent Blue Ridge Mountains.

Vera chuckled. "Eventually we did, but we almost didn't have a screened porch! You see," she continued, "we didn't agree on how to go about it. The problem was that David's favorite tree was right here in the middle of where the porch needed to go. I wanted to cut it down. David didn't. I still remember the conversation:

'Vera,' David said, 'how could we even consider cutting down this tree? It's older than we are!'

'If we want to build our porch,' I replied to David, 'the tree will have to go. There simply isn't another spot for it.'

"Back and forth we went, each desperately wanting our own way. Finally David capitulated. Giving me a gift of love, he said, 'We shall cut down the tree. You shall have your screened porch!'"

Did David ever regret giving in to you?" I (Claudia) asked.

Vera laughed, "No, not at all! You see, when the tree came down, we discovered it was hollow. The inside had rotted away. It was good riddance! And if David had insisted on keeping the tree, in its weakened state, a wind storm could have blown it over on our home."

Then we realized how that tree is like marriage . . . *selfishness leads to decay; deferring to the other leads to blessing.*

Just as Vera and David's tree appeared to be fine, our marriage may look great on the outside, but if we selfishly demand our own way, our marriage will decay on the inside. Over time, our relationship can become hollow, weak and rotten. But when we defer to each other, we strengthen our relationship.

Years later when we remember Vera's tree story, we are challenged to work on our marriage—to cut down our own trees of selfishness and to defer to the other. Then we can help other couples build better marriages, and hopefully in the sunset of our lives, we will also enjoy rocking on our own screened porch.

What do we live for, if it is not to make life less difficult for each other?

GEORGE ELIOT

THIRTY-FIVE

Call Unto Me

Ben and Austin stared at each across the table. Suddenly Ben realized how far apart they had drifted. They didn't even agree about their recent move to the West Coast. Austin missed her close-knit family in New England. Ben just didn't understand.

"Why can't you be more supportive?" he asked. This was his opportunity to move into the leadership of a national ministry. After all, this wasn't just a job, it was a calling.

Austin reminded him. "But, it's not my calling! I miss my home, my friends. I feel so alone." The stress of moving a family of five all the way across the United States had taken its toll. Tears welled up in Austin's eyes.

Ben stared in helpless silence. They knew each other so well—and yet they were strangers. "How have we gotten so disconnected?" Ben asked.

"I don't know," Austin answered. "But I do know deep down we love each other. Surely we can work things out."

The one thing they did agree on that morning was that they wanted to start over—to begin again. But how? In Maine they had always been so close—especially when they took time to pray together. Now that seemed impossible—or was it? Did God understand? Could their Heavenly Father help them bridge the chasm that separated them?

Sheepishly Ben said, "We could try praying together. That used to help."

Austin wiping away the tears, looked at Ben with a faint glimmer of hope. "We can give it a try. We certainly don't have anything to lose."

Ben reached for Austin's hand and began to pray, "God, if you are here, we need your help."

And then God impressed upon them, *I am always here. You are the one who moved—not just away from Maine—but also away from Me. I am always ready to listen, to hear your prayers and to meet the deepest needs of your hearts. Don't hold back. Call unto Me and I will restore you and renew your marriage.*

Together they poured out their fears and concerns to each other and to God. And in the silence, they connected at a deeper level. Heart to heart they renewed their commitment to each other and to God.

In the coming weeks, they would live out their commitment in practical ways—like listening to each other when one would rather go to sleep and putting the other first through little daily acts of kindness, or mounting a concerted effort to replace a negative thought with a positive one. And in those times when they disagreed or began to experience self-pity, they would stop and listen for God's voice. And as they prayed together they would again discover God's refreshment for the soul of their marriage.

Do not worry about anything; instead pray about everything; tell God your needs and don't forget to thank him for his answers.
PHILIPPIANS 4:8 (TLB)

THIRTY-SIX

In Pain and In Joy

He held her close as she gently sobbed. Unspoken words. She squeezed his hand—each seeking to comfort the other.

Such highs. Such lows. The excitement, "We're going to be parents!" Unspeakable joy. A glorious future. A child's laugh to be. Awe. The continuation of the cycle of life!

Then the unfathomable words—"miscarriage"— the death of a baby yet to be born. Doctors, hospitals, tears, the reality of what would never be. They held each other, partners in pain. Then in the midst of their suffering God comforted them . . . *You do not need to understand the past or the present to trust Me with the future. I know the plans I have for you—they are for your good so that you may have hope.*

Days turned into weeks. Weeks turn into months. God's promise became the salve that soothed the pain.

Time passes. Years go by. The scene changes. God's plan unfolds.

Once again they rush to the hospital. Breathe! Breathe! Relax! Breathe! Push! Push! A child is born. A new life is given. A new future created. Hope realized is a tree of life. The couple rejoices. A baby gasps for air and cries. The cycle of life continues.

Hope deferred makes the heart sick,
But a longing fulfilled is a tree of life.
PROVERBS 13:12

THIRTY-SEVEN

Follow the Light

What should have been a lovely drive through the Austrian Alps was not. Instead we could see nothing—just miles and miles of fog. We had looked forward to driving back to Zurich, Switzerland, to catch our ten-hour flight home, but we had not anticipated this fog.

Then, near Innsbruck, the dreary sky hiding the Alps gradually became brighter and brighter, and in one magic moment the fog at the very top of the Alps broke. We could finally see the tip of the Alps. The next moment they disappeared—as if they were playing hide and seek with us. Fog. Alps. Fog. Alps.

How breathtaking it was when the fog lifted and we could see the majesty of the Alps! How disappointing when the thick fog reappeared! But isn't this how life is sometimes? Or even, on occasions, our marriage? At times we see so clearly the beauty all around us—and at other times we only see the fog. Yet, like the Alps in the fog, the beauty is always there whether we can see it or not!

As we continued to drive toward Innsbruck, we talked about times we have felt close to God and other times when we felt only distance. And then God seemed to speak to our hearts: *Like the Alps, I am there even when you don't see Me! Trust Me in the foggy times as well as the sunny times in your life and in your marriage.*

Oh, if we could only remember this lesson—especially when we're in a fog of discouragement. God is there in the foggy times just as He is there when all is sunny in our lives. We need to trust Him both times.

And then as we approached the outskirts of Innsbruck, the sun suddenly broke through. Suddenly, we were surrounded by God's majesty—360 degrees of magnificent stately Alps! We promised each other we would remember this day and in those times when fog reappears, we will remind each other that in the midst of the darkness and dullness, God is still there—even when we don't feel His presence! His love and protection—more majestic than the Alps—surrounds us!

As the mountains surround Jerusalem,
So the Lord surrounds his people both now and forever.
PSALM 125:2

THIRTY-EIGHT

Courageous Risks

When we moved to our condo, we wanted to add a few trees as a privacy buffer. Our friend, Radio, agreed to help plant them for us. Since we were leaving for a conference, we took Radio's suggestion and left our new trees just where we wanted them planted.

Soon after we left, a huge storm raced through. When Radio came to plant the new trees, they were somewhat in the area we wanted them planted even though the storm had rearranged them. That part worked out fine, but our tropical ficus tree had blown off the deck—and Radio planted it, too!

The prognosis for a tropical plant surviving a cold winter is not good. So after several more weeks of glorying in the fall sunshine—and, we might add, thriving—we replanted our ficus tree in a larger pot. After giving it a few days to acclimatize, we moved our tree inside for the winter. The results? It's never been so healthy! Being uprooted and replanted was like a shot of vitamins for our little tree.

As we laughed about our ficus tree, we thought about our marriage. Could our ficus story represent what God so often does with us? Just when we start to get complacent, he sends something—even storms—into our lives to stir us up. He replants us!

And then God spoke to our hearts . . . *Change is inevitable, growth is optional. The changes and even the storms of life can cause you to grow closer together. Don't settle for a root-bound marriage!*

At that moment we realized that even mistakes can shake us out of complacency and jump-start growth. Our ficus tree is a living example.

And what did we do with the hole vacated by our ficus tree? We found a more appropriate holly tree to take its place, but each time we see it, it reminds us of our ficus tree's days in the sun. It reminds us to never give up adventure. To take the risk of growing and, rather than becoming root-bound, to let our roots grow deep in God's love, to lift our marriage branches toward heaven and let the storms of life continue to challenge us to grow closer to each other.

Courageous risks are life giving, they help you grow, make you brave and better than you think you are.
MARIE CURIE

THIRTY-NINE

Seize the Day

We met Carlos and Genie at our church's mission conference. Their enthusiasm, energy and sheer joy of living drew us to them. Parents of two young daughters and missionaries in Mexico, they were interested in helping marriages and families. They were especially fascinated with our concept of 10 Great Dates®.

"When we get back to Mexico," Carlos told us, "we will start our own 10 Great Dates group." Assuring us they would stay in touch, we said good-bye, looking forward to hearing from them in the future.

So you can imagine our shock when the next November we received a letter from Carlos telling us that Genie had died suddenly of meningitis. Now, his life was turned upside down—he was alone with his two young daughters.

As our mission conference rolled around that spring, we wondered if Carlos would be there. He was, and he sent word that he wanted to talk with us. We'll never forget that conversation.

Carlos told us how he and Genie started their own Great Dates group and how they kept each other's children so each couple could have their dates. It really worked! Their dates were fun, refreshing and reenergizing for their marriage. Then he told us about the last week of Genie's life.

"That week it was our time for others to keep our children. So on Sunday we had our Great Date. We walked and talked and just enjoyed being together. The next day I left for an out-of-town conference. When I kissed Genie goodbye, I had no clue it would be that last time I would hold her in my arms. Soon after I left, she became ill and in a matter of hours she was gone.

"Tell other couples," Carlos told us with his voice breaking, "not to take each other for granted, to seize the day, to take time for their marriages now. You just don't know how long you will have with each other."

Our eyes filled with tears. We thought of the past week. We had been busy. Too busy. We had missed our weekly date. Then God seemed to whisper to us . . . *Seize the day for your marriage! Not tomorrow, not next week, next month or next year! Seize the day today!*

Fortunately, our story has a happy ending. Carlos came back to the United States with his two daughters. Time heals. Life goes on. Sandy, another missionary who also had a heart for Mexico, entered his life. Love blossomed. Now, back in Mexico, Carlos and Sandy are partners in marriage and ministry and parents to the two girls. They have regular dates. They work at keeping their own relationship growing and fresh. They keep on *"seizing the day!"* Can we do less? Heaven forbid, but it could be all that we have!

See each morning as if it were the morning of the very first day; treasure each day as if it were the evening of the very last day.
ANONYMOUS

FORTY

Monday Morning Coffee

Jennifer poured another cup of coffee. "Maybe the caffeine will kick in soon," she mumbled to herself. The hectic weekend was over, and here she was facing another Monday morning—another week of being both mom and dad to her three preschoolers. Not exactly the way she and Collin had pictured family life years ago, when the greatest crisis was how to make it through the month on their meager budget.

Finances were no longer the major source of stress in their marriage. Instead, the present stress was Collin's job. Being a successful marketing consultant required him to be an absentee dad and husband for most of the week, Monday through Friday. The next rung on Collin's career ladder should require less travel, but for now, extensive traveling was just part of the landscape.

Jennifer thought of Collin. That morning he had slipped out early before she woke up. She didn't even get to kiss him good-bye. Now he was somewhere in the sky between Dallas and Los Angeles and would not return until Friday, when another whirlwind weekend would greet them. Then the cycle would repeat itself. And just as the kids readjusted to having Dad home again, the weekend would be gone and Collin would head for the airport.

Jennifer loved being a mom. She realized that life is lived in seasons, that now was her opportunity to impact these young lives. She also loved Collin, but as she faced another week as a single parent, she was discouraged and felt so alone. How can I make it through another week? She honestly didn't know. Then she felt God's unmistakable presence and His assurance, *You can make it through this week one moment at a time. You are not alone. I am with you. Life is lived in moments. Trust Me to give you the strength and courage for this time in your life. I have called you to love and nurture your children and to partner with Collin. Together you can surmount the challenges of this season of your lives.*

Slowly, as Jennifer sipped her coffee, she reminded herself, *this crazy schedule is just for a season. Collin's traveling won't go on forever. The boys will grow up. I can choose to live moment-by-moment, to love and nurture our sons, and to love and support Collin. Our love can deepen through partnering together even with miles between us.*

Her thoughts were interrupted by a gentle tug on her bathrobe. "Mommy, will you read me a book?" Billy, her oldest son, looked up at her expectantly. "Sure I will," she replied. Billy threw his arms around her, and in that hug she discovered the energy she needed for the moment. Then she realized: her Heavenly Father would provide the strength for every future moment—for this day, this week and the weeks to come.

> *The Lord gives strength to his people;*
> *the Lord blesses his people with peace.*
> PSALMS 29:11

FORTY-ONE

Unfriendly Skies

Y ou'll have to check your luggage in at the airline counter inside," the curb-side porter said. Another cancelled flight. Another delay. Exhausted after leading a weekend seminar, we were very ready to get home. We looked at each other and sighed. "Are we having fun yet?" Dave asked.

Fun wasn't exactly how I (Claudia) would describe this rather frustrating situation. Besides, it was my birthday, and I wanted to celebrate it at home. Now we were going to be several hours late getting there. Unfortunately, airport delays are all too familiar for us. Leading seminars around the country, cancelled and delayed flights just come with our job. But that day it was more exasperating because it was my birthday. I was tired and just wanted to go home.

Finally we boarded another flight . . . and sat alone. On top of everything else, they couldn't give us seats together. I silently asked, "Why today, of all days?"

Then, just as the plane started racing down the runway, I heard an almost audible answer, *Why not today?* Then silence.

"Because it's my birthday! I want to get home!" I silently argued.

Then God reminded me, *If life were totally predictable—totally on schedule—think how boring it would be! Delays, change of plans and cancellations are part of the fabric of life. My child, relax. Trust Me. I hold the master plan for your life. Flights can and will be cancelled and delayed, but I will never be late or forsake you. Trust Me with your life . . . trust Me with your marriage . . . trust Me today with your birthday.*

The plane left the ground and climbed through the clouds into the brilliant rays of the sun. I pushed the seat recliner button, put my head back, and relaxed. If airport delays were just part of life, perhaps I should embrace them. After all, the flight, though a rescheduled one, was taking us home.

Soon we would be sitting side-by-side on our screened porch. There would be plenty of time to celebrate our unpredictable—and definitely not boring—life, to celebrate our marriage, and at long last, to celebrate my birthday. I decided to relax. After all . . . I would have a whole year before turning another year older!

Be strong and courageous. Do not be terrified; do not be discouraged, for the Lord your God will be with you wherever you go.

JOSHUA 1:9

FORTY-TWO

Slow Down, Be Renewed

Here we were again in Austria for a short pre-Christmas break to relax and get in tune with each other and with the Lord before the hustle and bustle of the holidays, and all the kids and grandkids descended upon us. But our time in Austria had not gone as planned. It had been one frustration after another.

It started when Avis gave us a car with summer tires. Hey, it's December! No surprise that didn't work out well for us in the snow and ice. We weren't able to make it up the icy hill to our chalet. We had no other choice than to carry our luggage, while slipping and sliding, up the ice-covered road. As we were unpacking and settling in, we soon discovered we had no Wi-Fi or internet connection. Zilch! Having forgone the expensive international plan for our note-book computers, we were limited to Wi-Fi. So much for streaming entertainment and keeping up with the news. (Obviously, we could do without the latter.) Our limited international data plan on our phones was—well, very limited!

Not a problem since we planned to spend lots of time outside, on the ski slopes and on winter snow hikes. But the weather wasn't cooperating either. Cold, Icy. No fresh snow. Everything looked dirty. The ski slopes—like the roads—were sheets of ice—so we stayed in by the open fire.

We slept, wrote Christmas cards and occasionally very carefully took walks in the icy snow and lugged groceries up the hill to our chalet. Like it or not, God had slowed us down. To be honest, we didn't like it.

On the last evening, would you believe it, started snowing. Really snowing. Fresh, lovely snow. Excited, we headed out for a night hike. We walked for an hour in the snow making a new path with each step we took. The new cover of snow illuminated the sky so we could see the peaceful village below, the farms on the rolling hills and the majestic Tyrolean Alps towering above us. Previously walking had been hard because of the ice, but with the new snow walking was effortless. Each step secure. No slipping or falling. Everything was beautiful.

With the softly falling snowflakes, God painted our world a beautiful white—seemingly just for us—no gaudy-colored Christmas tree lights nor Santas climbing chimneys; no commercials shouting "Buy me!"; no ringing phones, no internet to surf; just a quiet whisper, *I brought you here to renew you—body and soul. And just as you're glorying in this walk in the new snow, I want you to go into this new year with joy and anticipation of what I have planned for you. Walk toward the Light and I will be with you every step of the way.*

Suddenly, all the frustrations of summer tires, cabin fever, ice and no Wi-Fi, were overshadowed by a realization that our Heavenly Father was renewing us—body and soul—and we could walk into the new year illuminated by His Light making a clear path for us follow. With a new sense of gratitude, we returned to our chalet to pack and prepare to head home the next morning.

Snowflakes are one of nature's most fragile things,
but just look at what they can do when they stick together.
VESTA M. KELLY

FORTY-THREE

The Gift of Love

A favorite song from our dating days is "Love Is a Many-Splendored Thing." It described the energy, enthusiasm, and excitement of our growing love for each other.

Perhaps you also remember the thrill of "young love," but over time things began to settle down. Did you, like us, discover that the person you thought was just about perfect also had some irritating habits? The stars in our eyes faded enough to see each other's little idiosyncrasies!

While love is still "a many splendored-thing," the reality of living together creates tension that can cloud the skies of romantic bliss. For instance, at times I (Dave) like my peace and quiet. There are times when I want to just chill out, check messages and spend some time on my notebook or watch a no-brainer movie, at the same time that Claudia really wants to talk. I can find it very frustrating! But just as

I'm ready to say, hey, can't we talk later, I hear a small, still voice, *Love is an attitude of caring more for the other person than caring for yourself. Can you turn this irritation into a gift of love by choosing to give her a gift of sacrifice and really listen to her—now?*

It works both ways, For instance, if I (Claudia) walk into the bathroom and there are Dave's clothes (from more than one day) draped over the tub rather than in the hamper or closet, I can become irritated—quickly—or I can give him a gift of love by simply hanging them up and choosing to see that act of kindness as my gift of service to Dave.

What about you? What about those times you're irritated with your spouse? Would you consider how you could turn your irritation into a gift of love? We all need reminders to love one another. And love is expressed in little acts of kindness.

We challenge you to think about what spells love to you. Are you willing to strive daily to choose the higher road of giving rather than receiving? Our prayer for you is that you will experience the joy of giving—not material gifts, but gifts of love, to the one whom you have chosen above all others to love and cherish.

Gifts of the heart—gifts of love—are gifts that last forever.

*Dear children, let us not love with words or tongue
but with actions and in truth.*
I JOHN 3:18

FORTY-FOUR

A Prodigal Marriage

Broken promises, deception, infidelity—Lila watched her marriage fall apart. Like the prodigal son, her husband Hal "set off for another life in a far country" and "squandered his wealth in wild living" (Luke 15:13). Most of Lila's friends advised her to divorce him, cut her losses and get on with her life. But like the father of the prodigal son, she refused to stop loving, caring and praying for Hal. She kept the porch light on—waiting for Hal to "come to his senses."

God answered Lila's prayers. Hal returned home repentant, remorseful and broken. "How could you let him walk all over you like this?" Lila's friends asked. And, like the father of the prodigal son, she answered, "Bring out the steaks. Light the grill. Let's celebrate! My marriage was dead; now it's alive again. My husband was lost and now he is found."

As we reflected on Lila and Hal, we wondered if we could be so forgiving, so loving, were we in Lila's situation. Then came the answer, *In your own power, no, but in my power and letting Me love through you, forgiveness, renewal, and hope for the future is more than possible! Remember, how much I have forgiven you!*

And what did Lila's and Hal's future hold for them? The reunion was only the beginning of this couple's efforts to rebuild their marriage and re-establish trust. It took time. It took hard work. There's no quick fix for a prodigal spouse. But Lila and Hal would never have salvaged their relationship if she hadn't forgiven him and given him a second chance.

Whether or not you have lived through marital pain like Lila and Hal, you've certainly felt wounded by your marriage partner at some point. Missed expectations. Unfulfilled dreams. Broken promises. These are a part of every marriage. The question is, "What marriage lessons can you learn about forgiveness from the story of the prodigal son? Are you willing to let go of your own hurts and disappointments, to forgive your spouse and choose to focus on the future? If so, the future of your marriage is bright.

Love is a fabric which never fades, no matter how often it is washed in the waters of adversity and grief.
ANONYMOUS

FORTY-FIVE

The Sands of Time

Side by side, hand in hand, we walk along the beach. We're not exactly dressed for the beach. Just having completed a six-hour marriage conference, we desperately need some down time—time to kick back and relax—but we forgot our jeans. What was that about our "all work and no play" mentality? Recently didn't one of our sons tell us to "get a life?" Here we are at one of the most beautiful beaches in Florida, and we didn't even think about packing beach clothes. Not to worry. We simply kicked off our shoes and rolled up our slacks. Now relaxing, we're walking on the beach.

The tide's coming in and chasing us as we try not to get wet. Before long our guard slips. The waves win. Our slacks are now wet and sandy. No need for further concern. We relax. Beaches do that to us. It's like our eyes and ears are opened. And our hearts. We pause to appreciate the rolling waves, the seagulls flying above. The birds standing on one leg. Other lovers passed by. At times like this, life slows down. We stop. Our eyes lock. We kiss. We look at each other through the filter of so many years of being soul mates, companions, lovers.

And then we see our delightful almost-twelve-month-old granddaughter, Lily. She sees the beach for the very first time. The glee. The delight. Her parents revel in the wonder of it all. Our son and daughter-in-law, here to help with our conference, are in their jeans and T-shirts—much better prepared for the beach than we are. As we reflect on this young couple we realize they are also better prepared to be parents. Better prepared to build a marriage. And then, as if we had heard an audible voice, we realize that . . . *life goes forward, not backwards . . . and just as constant as the sands of time, our Heavenly Father goes forward with us. Just as constant as the waves of the ocean, His love will always encompass us.*

We think of our own sons, their wives, our grandchildren, including precious Lily, who is named after Dave's mom. Yet, even now I (Dave) remember my parents, in years gone by, walking on the beach, hand in hand. Kissing. Then I was the child. Today, I'm the husband, the dad, the granddad. Life goes forward.

We pause and together we pray, *"Please let us be a positive marriage model for our children and grandchildren. May we leave a path of healthy relationships for them to follow in the sands of time."*

I will surely bless you and make your descendants as numerous as the stars in the sky and as the sand on the seashore.
GENESIS 22:24

ABOUT THE AUTHORS

Claudia Arp and David Arp, MSW, founders of Marriage Alive International, Inc., share a passion for helping couples build great marriages through fun, relationship-building dates. The Arps introduced the dating concept when dating wasn't cool. Today their *10 Great Dates*® brand of resources including books, DVD-based programs and seminars, are popular nationally and internationally. They have authored over 30 books including the award-winning *The Second Half of Marriage*. More about the Arps at www.10greatdates.org.

SPEAKING TOPICS

The Ultimate Great Date Night
Fun in Marriage is Serious Business

Turtle and Skunk on a Date (Dealing with conflict in a positive way)
Seminars:
The Marriage Alive Seminar
10 Great Dates - The Seminar
The Second Half of Marriage Seminar
Suddenly They're 13 - or the Art of Hugging a Cactus

ALSO AVAILABLE FROM DAVID & CLAUDIA ARP:

Books

10 Great Dates to Energize Your Marriage

10 Great Dates for Empty Nesters

10 Great Dates Before You Say "I Do"

10 Great Dates: Connecting Faith, Love and Marriage (co-authored with Heather and Peter Larson)

$10 Great Dates (co-authored with Heather and Peter Larson)

52 Fantastic Dates for You and Your Mate

The Second Half of Marriage

Fighting for Your Empty Nest Marriage (co-authored with Scott Stanley, Howard Markman, and Susan Blumberg)

No Time for Sex

She's Almost a Teenager—Essential Conversations to Have Now (co-authored with Heather and Peter Larson)

The Connected Family

Suddenly They're 13—or the Art of Hugging a Cactus

Answering the 8 Cries of the Spirited Child

Video Curriculum

10 Great Dates to Energize Your Marriage

10 Great Dates Before You Say "I Do" (with Heather and Peter Larson)

Great Dates Connect (with Heather and Peter Larson)

The Second Half of Marriage

ABOUT THE PUBLISHER

FH Publishers is a division of FaithHappenings.com

FaithHappenings.com is the premier, first-of-its kind, online Christian resource that contains an array of valuable local and national faith-based information all in one place. Our mission is "to inform, enrich, inspire and mobilize Christians and churches while enhancing the unity of the local Christian community so they can better serve the needs of the people around them." FaithHappenings.com will be the primary iPhone, Droid App/Site and website that people with a traditional Trinitarian theology will turn to for national and local information to impact virtually every area of life.

The vision of FaithHappenings.com is to build the vibrancy of the local church with a true "one-stop-resource" of information and events that will enrich the soul, marriage, family, and church life for people of faith. We want people to be touched by God's Kingdom, so they can touch others FOR the Kingdom.

To learn more, visit www.faithhappenings.com.

www.ingramcontent.com/pod-product-compliance
Lightning Source LLC
Chambersburg PA
CBHW031556040426
42452CB00006B/321